Venice, Italy
Coloring Book

Nick Snels

ColoringArtist.com

You can find angel flower girls, animals, Aztec, Christmas, Easter, Halloween, horses, mandala, mermaid, alphabet, numbers, pirates, skylines, Valentine's Day, Venetian Carnival masks, ... coloring books at http://www.coloringartist.com

Copyright © 2015 - Nick Snels
http://www.coloringartist.com

All rights reserved. No part of this publication may be reproduced, distributed, or transmitted in any form or by any means, including photocopying, recording, or other electronic or mechanical methods. All images are licensed acquired and remain copyright to their respective owners. Images © BORTEL Pavel - Pavelmidi/Shutterstock.com, IR Stone/Shutterstock.com, Mikhail Bakunovich/Shutterstock.com, silverjohn/Shutterstock.com, Viktoriya/Shutterstock.com, Yoko Design/Shutterstock.com

Rialto Bridge

Doge's courtyard building

Basilica San Marco

Doge's Palace

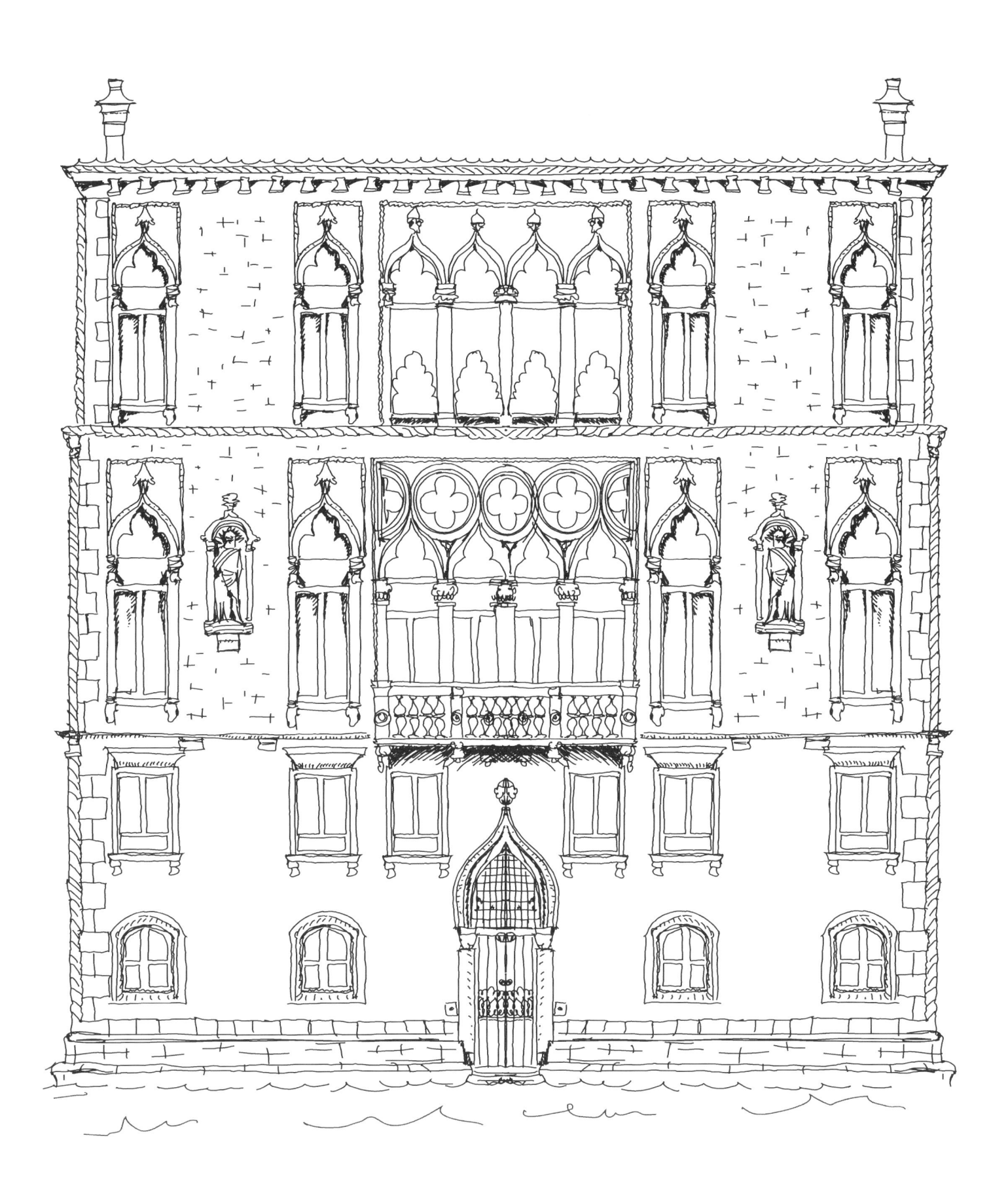

Grand Canal private house

Rialto Bridge

12.27.15

Saint Mark's Campanile and the Doge's Palace

Doge's Palace

Venice

San Marco Lion

Rialto Bridge

Venice

San Marco Lion

Venice water canal, old buildings and gondola

Venetian carnaval mask

12.27.15

Island of San Giorgio Maggiore

Grand Canal, with a view on the Rialto Bridge

Grand Canal, with a view on the Rialto Bridge

Calle Fondamenta Megio

Grand Canal. Ancient building and gondola

Cathedral of Santa Maria della Salute

Fondamenta Rio Marin

Piazza San Marco and Kampanila. View from the Doge's Palace

Calle Frutarol

Ponte del Mondo Novo, Campo S. Maria Formosa

Ancient buildings and canal with gondola

Gondola at the pier

Piazza San Marco. Capitals of columns of Doge's Palace

Grand Canal, with a view on the Rialto Bridge

Grand Canal

Grand Canal

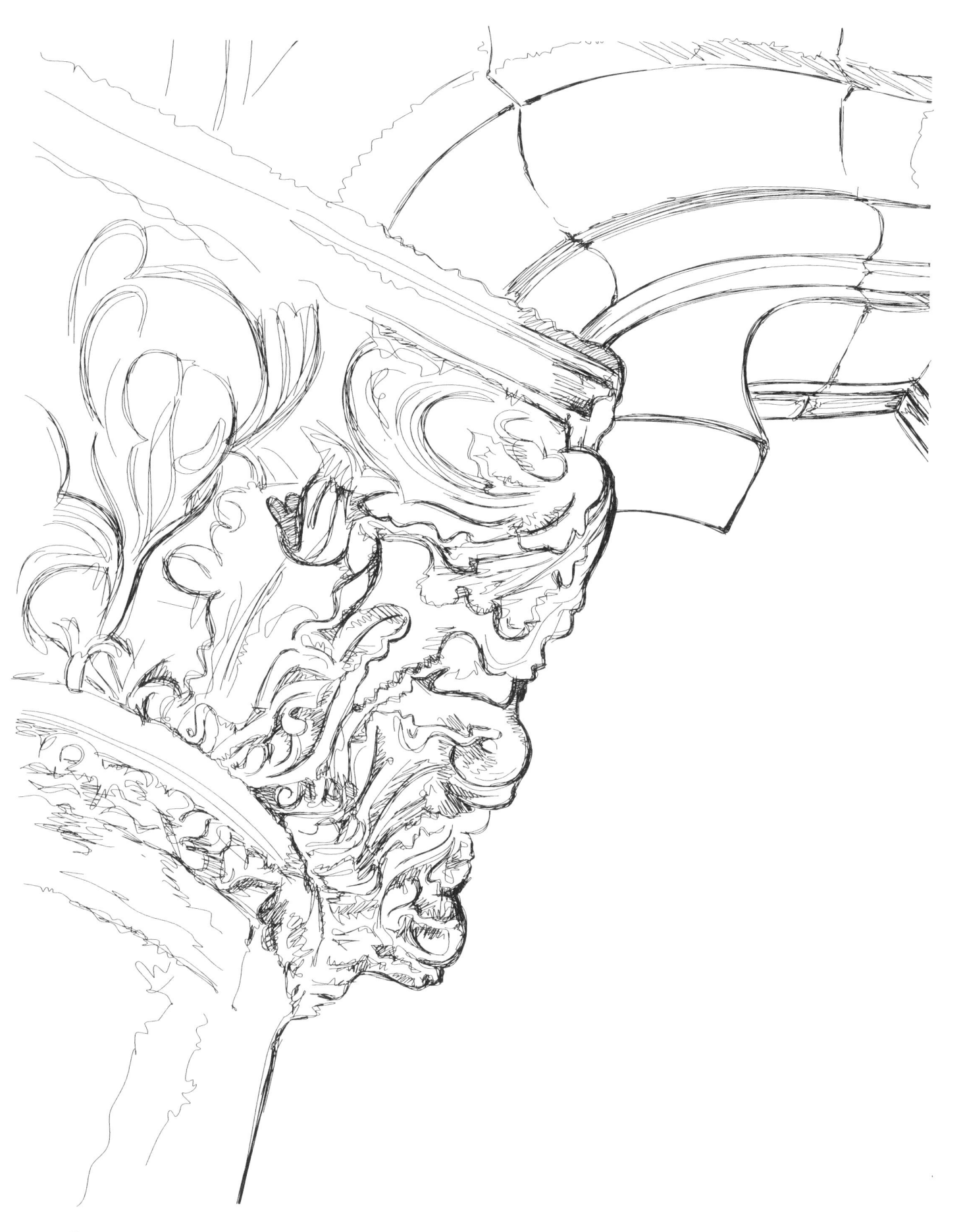

Piazza San Marco. Capitals of a column of Doge's Palace

Piazza San Marco. Capitals of columns of Doge's Palace

Piazza San Marco and Kampanila. View from the Doge's Palace

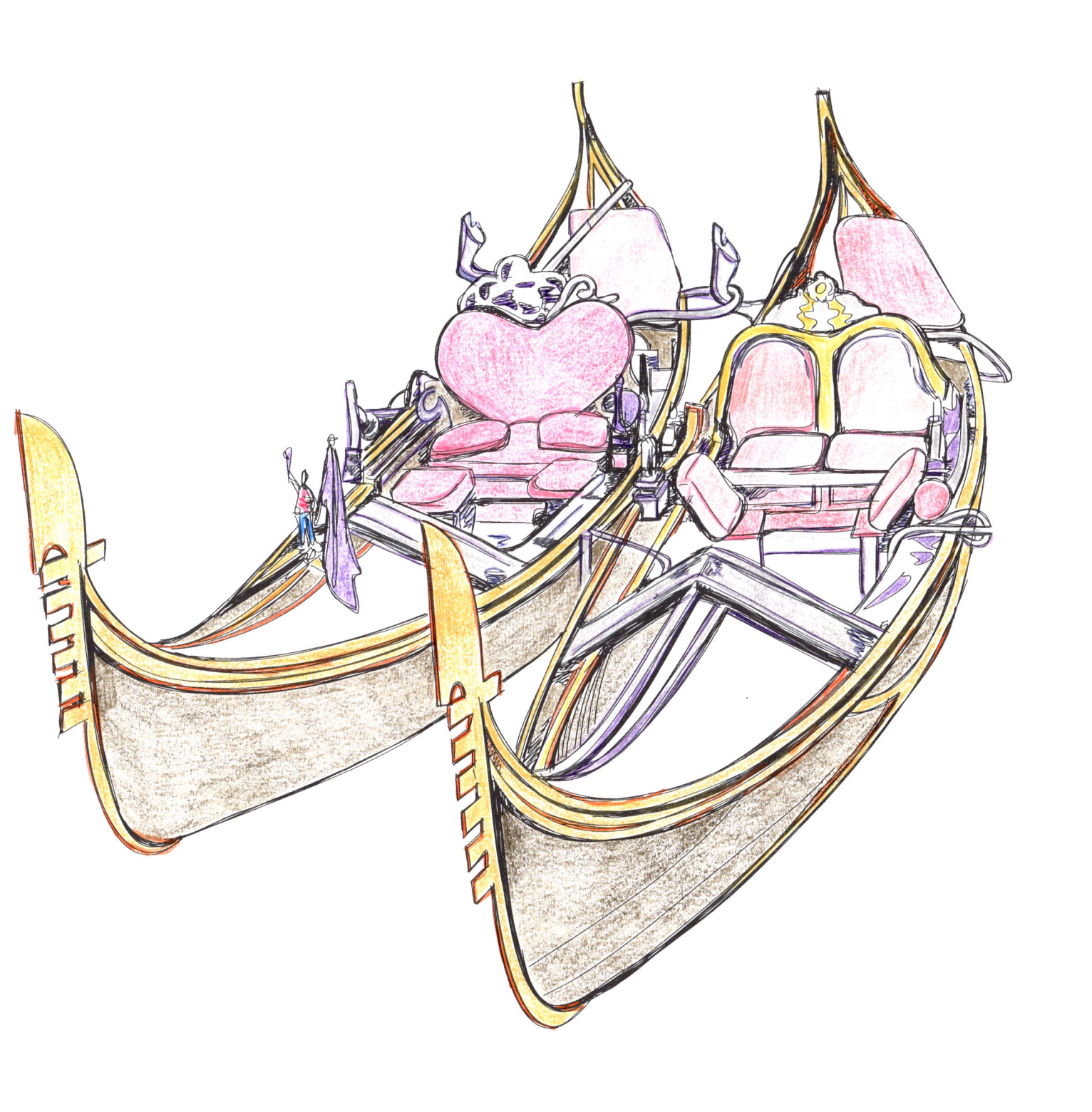

Two gondolas

12.26.15

Grand Canal

Calle Fondamenta Megio

Fondamenta Rio Marin

Piazza San Marco. Columns of the Doge's Palace

Grand Canal, with a view on the Rialto Bridge

View of the Grand Canal near the Rialto Bridge

Ponte del Mondo Novo, Campo S. Maria Formosa

Grand Canal. View of the Rialto Bridge

Piazza San Marco, Doge's Palace and a view of the island of San Giorgio Maggiore

Island of San Giorgio Maggiore

Quay Piazza San Marco

Piazza San Marco. Lantern on St. Mark's Square and corner of the Doge's Palace

Piazza San Marco. A view of the island of San Giorgio Maggiore

Quay Piazza San Marco

12.27.15

Grand Canal, with a view on the Rialto Bridge

Skylines of the United
States Coloring Book

Venetian Carnival
Masks Coloring Book 1

Angel Flower Girl
Coloring Book 1

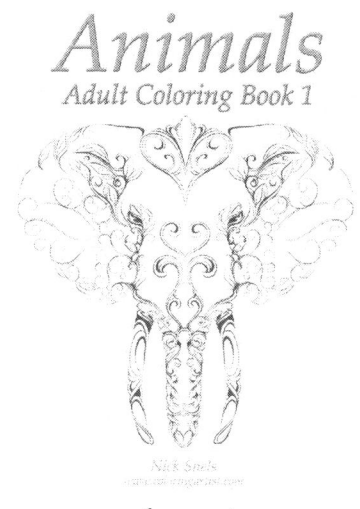

Animals
Adult Coloring Book 1

Aztec
Coloring Book

Bible
Coloring Book 1

Cute Kittens and Cats
Coloring Book 1

Horses, Unicorns and
Pegasus Adult Coloring Book

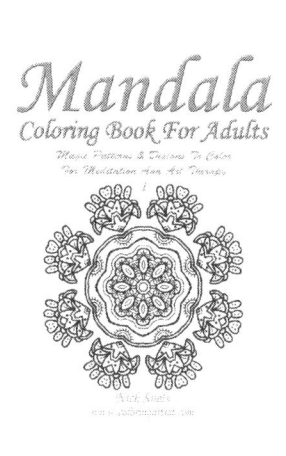

Mandala Coloring
Book For Adults 1

*Please post a positive review on Amazon,
if you loved this coloring book.*

Thank you,

Nick

Made in the USA
Lexington, KY
02 December 2015